Staying Motivated

The Ultimate Guide to Staying Motivated While at Work

Table of Contents

Introduction

I want to thank you and congratulate you for downloading the book "Staying Motivated

The Ultimate Guide to Staying Motivated While at Work"

Sometimes, at work, your inspiration may get totally exhausted. However, circumstances direct that you can't stop. So how would you continue onward? There's dependably a way.

It's unavoidable. As time passes, at any employment, you have a day that truly sucks. At that point, in the long run, perhaps another. Furthermore, another. All of a sudden the occupation you cherished begins to feel like, well, work. What's more, awful work at that. It doesn't need to be that way.

Much like the vast majority, we all confronted different cases where there was nothing keeping us at a job, yet bills and obligations implied stopping wasn't an alternative either. In such cases, it's hard to show up, not to mention do your work to your best capacity.

In any case, there are steps that have made a difference

This book contains proven steps and strategies on how motivate yourself or push yourself when you are demotivated.

Let's take a look shall we?

Chapter 1: It Could Be Your Fault?

We've all managed with terrible supervisors or lesser paycheck than we'd like, however that doesn't mean the cure for your problems includes leaving your place of employment and finding another. Each occupation is still work, and each employment accompanies drawbacks. They call it "work" for a reason, and regardless of the fact that you're fortunate and do what you adore, you'll have awful days, and it can in any case suck some of the time.

Despite everything you'll need to deal with managers who boss you around, know-it-all associates, and, now and again, disappointing busywork. Indeed, even thus, a hefty portion of us hop between occupations with just a short time after our first day until we definitely finish up "this employment sucks!" and begin searching for the following one.

So how would you beat back that disturbing sensation that your job is going to, in the long run, end up sucking?

Indeed, numerous circumstances warrant leaving your place of employment. In the event that it truly is an ideal opportunity to walk out, you ought to do it. This eBook is for whomever decides to stay. Here, we'll walk you through some tips to stay engaged, peppy, and content with your work—particularly on the off chance that the work pulled in you to an occupation in any case.

Check Yourself

The first and most intense thing you can do immediately is to change your outlook. There are a lot of approaches to go about this, however it begins with understanding that you have the last say over how you feel. Nobody can make you feel second rate without your opinion and the reason applies here. You will be unable to prevent inescapable working environment irritations from happening, yet you can prevent them from destroying your day.

Here's the means by which:

- **Avoid Water Cooler Talk and Gossip**

In the event that everybody in your specialty thinks everything sucks, you're prone to feel the same way, regardless of the possibility that you don't have anything to grumble about. Attempt to stay target when conversing with colleagues about working environment issues and office governmental issues, and don't give the babble a chance to get to you. Concentrate on your work, and doing the best work you can.

- **Oppose Negativity**

Maintaining a strategic distance from gossip is a decent initial step, however you can likewise be a piece of the arrangement. Search for the positive and talk it up to colleagues. Make a rundown of those positive parts of your employment and keep it up front each day. Maybe you get the chance to take a shot at something you adore, or your occupation offers you training for free, or all the espresso you can drink. Whatever makes you grin about your occupation, ensure you see and exploit it each and every day.

- **Search for More Perks**

What number of your employment's advantages do you make utilization of? Search hard for them, and exploit them as frequently as could reasonably be expected. Whether it's adaptable hours or an easygoing workplace, turn your employment from a spot you go each day to a dynamic piece of your life that adds to your wellbeing past your paycheck.

- **Figure Out How to Adapt**

Anxiety will dependably discover you—There is no job where you don't find stress. The imperative thing is to figure out how anxiety influences you and what you can do about it. Take up a diversion, contemplate, guide somebody at work—whatever it takes. As you build up those methods for dealing with stress, you'll be less disposed to hating your employment all in all. Forcefully search them out, as well. When something pesters you, quickly consider how you can address the anxiety, regardless of the fact that you can't address the issue.

The Importance of Perspective

At the point when your employment gets you down, it places things in context. Without a doubt, there are things about your employment that make you hopeless, yet every occupation will have a few components that aren't perfect. The imperative thing to do is particular those things out from the things that make you glad.

The imperative thing to ask yourself: Are these bothering things my genuine employment, identified with my real occupation, or simply encompassing my employment?

On the off chance that they're a piece of your real occupation, let your supervisor recognize what's irritating you. In case you're stuck taking a shot at a maturing stage that makes you hopeless in light of the fact that it goes as the week progressed, your manager may concur that it's an ideal opportunity to supplant it—particularly since you must be backing that framework.

In the event that those aggravations are encompassing components, you ought to hunt down answers for those things as well, however remember that they're not illustrative of the employment itself. On the off chance that you appreciate what you do, don't give the little stuff a chance to trouble you. Concentrate on the work and manage the little stuff as an afterthought.

Taking Responsibility

Inspiration is natural. While other components influence it, your response to those elements is the thing that at last will leave you demotivated. Be that as it may, there's a distinction between assuming liability for this and pointing the finger at yourself for this—and unreasonably regularly, we choose to blame ourselves.

We've all chided ourselves for not pushing harder and improving. Be that as it may, it's a fleeting example of overcoming adversity. Once the task is completed we fall again into depression. On the off chance that your occupation sucks, it may be your flaw; however, assume liability for that and alter it instead of upbraiding and disgracing yourself.

We're urged to be liable to uplift ourselves. It can be terrifying, yet the quality of it feels incredible. When we take responsibility for our life and there's an issue, we are responsible for the solution. It's your decision. This can be uplifting news to some

Also we don't need to sit tight for another person to change, or for a condition to change – none of which we can control. So taking personal responsibility helps you out.

Be that as it may, during the time spent doing that, without anyone else's help blame can inch in, without our knowledge.

The following is what self-blame says:

- "I have to settle myself"
- "I have to rebuff myself somehow"
- "I have to lament about what I did"

Then again, assuming liability essentially obliges you to see your part in what's going on. We can do this sincerely and can look past the initial self-blame.

Instead, at that point simply ask yourself: "Do I need to change something? Provided that this is true, what are a few choices? What activity do I have to take to change things?"

This keeps you in a looking-forward position – concentrated on what's to come. Also, it will get you started with a direction to move in.

On the off chance that that is what you're considering, then you need to escape that undesirable spot. Assume liability by recognizing your mix-ups and gaining from them. It's harder and requires more investment, however it's dependable.

You can just gain from a mistake after you admit you've made it. When you begin accusing other individuals (or the universe itself), you separate yourself from any conceivable lesson. Be that as it may, in the event that you fearlessly stand up and genuinely own-up and say "This is my misstep and I am capable" the potential outcomes for learning will move towards you.

Affirmation of an error, regardless of the fact that exclusive secretly to yourself, makes learning conceivable by moving the concentrate far from accuse task and towards understanding. Shrewd individuals concede their mix-ups effectively. They know progress quickens when they do.

Gaining from mistakes requires three things:

- Placing yourself in circumstances where you can commit intriguing errors
- Having the fearlessness to admit to them
- Being courageous about changing

Chapter 2: Coping with Demotivation

Inspiration is in actuality an essential part of making progress in the work environment. It is the undetectable vitality that pushes you to make a special effort, keep your center, and accomplish your objectives. Without it, it's difficult to feel a feeling of satisfaction.

More terrible, its belongings aren't just restricted to yourself. Poor efficiency as a result of your absence of inspiration can truly influence the path others around you carry out their occupations. It likewise makes an effect on your association's main concern.

Demotivation, or the demonstration of losing the drive to push forward, is a genuine worry that should be tended to at the soonest time conceivable. It is important to get to the base of your disappointment keeping in mind the end goal to outline a powerful diagram intended to bring you back on track.

Here are a portion of the basic reasons for being demotivated:

- **Unfulfilled desires**

  At the point when your amazing dreams of how things should function end up being a flop, you feel a feeling of frustration assume control you, bringing about absence of interest and inspiration to bear on not surprisingly. You feel ripped off and you stop caring.

- **Boredom**

  On the off chance that you are left with an undertaking that does not provoke you, then you start to slack off and take things delicately.

- **Lack of Motivating Forces**

  Let's be honest: cash is an awesome inspiration. Furthermore, an intense one, as well. The possibility of procuring loads of money subsequent to finishing your assignments serves as a remunerating background that exclusive attests your avidness to work harder whenever. With no type of motivator toward the end of the pipeline, it's difficult to get inspired in light of the fact that, paying little mind to how you fared, there's nothing in it for you at any rate.

- **Poor** **administration**

There's no awesome De-motivator very like an administration that does not treat its representatives decently or others consciously.

- **Frustrations as a Result of Having an Excessive Number of Tenets to Take After**

Studies demonstrate that the happiest representatives are frequently the individuals who are given a specific feeling of self-governance to do their capacities.

- **Stress**

There are sure errands that are just much excessively intricate, tedious, and hard to finish in one go. The dissatisfaction that comes as a consequence of this trouble frequently shows signs of improvement of some individuals, who choose it's a great deal more advantageous to simply surrender out and out as opposed to go ahead.

Generally, demotivation can be cured by cultivating a more positive mentality about work. For instance, rather than looking at work as a chore in as an errand, consider it an important approach to strengthen your insight and abilities, which will most likely be helpful once you ascend the work and social stepping stool later on.

Rather than considering it a discipline, highlight its remunerating viewpoints, for example, the opportunity to work with awesome individuals, the chance to exhibit your thoughts, or the opportunity to procure cash that can pay your bills. Be that as it may, it's not about the cash, see. Truth be told, in case you're feeling demotivated, now might be as great a period as any to evaluate your needs and reevaluate your objectives.

Re-Examine Goals

In making objectives, recall to be specific. As it were, know precisely what you need to accomplish. On the off chance that an objective looks excessively intricate, separate it into a progression of sensible parts. Case in point, if you will probably complete a task, you can really separate this further into littler objectives.

Completing the exploration, gathering information, displaying the paper, making proposals, and actualizing adjustments are only a portion of the undertakings that constitute the sum of the venture. It's likewise great to compose your objectives in light of a particular arrangement of criteria, for example, promptness, significance, measure of assets required, and level of trouble, among others.

This will permit you to see which objectives to organize and help you keep yourself from superfluously immersed with an excessive amount of undertakings all in the meantime. Lastly, draw an unmistakable, reasonable, and totally down to business timetable for your objectives.

Making due dates for every errand that you are setting yourself up for legitimizes the entire thing and pushes you to work harder. The possibility that you need to beat due dates is an awesome method for rousing yourself to get moving.

Managing Stress

Another method for overcoming demotivation at work is by having the capacity to legitimately oversee and manage stress. A typical working environment grumbling, stress evokes a large group of negative sentiments which, when left unchecked, can be exceptionally crippling.

Truth be told, it's not unprecedented to watch a failure to focus and an inclination to make misrepresented reactions among the individuals who are under enormous anxiety. Simultaneously, their efficiency and association with other individuals likewise get strained rather pointlessly.

Thankfully, there are two or three snappy anxiety administration methods that should be possible once you feel that push is starting to show signs of improvement of you.

Here are some of them:

- **Take deep and relaxing breaths**

  Profound inward breaths through the nostrils completed by long exhalations the mouth have a speedy quieting impact. Doing this a couple times backs off the rate of your pulse and instantly quiets down your nerves.

- **Listen to Music**

  Music is known for its restorative impact. Make a playlist of tunes that lift up your spirits, unwind you, or keep you centered. Listen to your most loved pop artists or get quiet with nature sounds, for example, ocean waves beating the shore or flying creatures peeping joyfully, and plan to abandon all your stresses.

- **Stare at anything green**

Studies show that when worried, taking a look at anything green sufficiently long can ease inside strain and make you feel more casual. This is the motivation behind why various organizations have their own green room, where worried workers can stay temporarily until they feel restored enough to resume what they were doing.

- **Squeeze a Stress Ball**

When you're worried, channel all your negative vitality toward an anxiety ball. This permits you to discharge repressed disappointments and negative vitality from your framework, helping you quiet down and feel lighter.

In whole, overcoming demotivation implies understanding where all your disappointment is originating from. This ought to be trailed by a reassessment of your needs and objectives, and in addition the capacity to manage stress. Most importantly, you need to figure out how to conform and trade off.

Chapter Three: Three Steps to Rid Your Demotivation

When you're demotivated, you impart aimlessly about things that trouble you. That can bring about a bigger number of issues than it tackles. We have built up a three-stage correspondence technique that helped me conquer demotivation. Vent, then evaluate, and after that discussion to the right individuals.

Vent

Venting your displeasure has been found to make you feel worse in the long haul. In any case, the old judgment skills maxim of venting having a transient cathartic impact is valid. The trick is to discover somebody you can dump your dissatisfactions on, however, you need to proceed onward to someone else. Somebody you trust has a discerning personality to understand those sentiments.

Discharging strain feels great. Hurling when you are debilitated feels great. At long last getting to a restroom feels great. Along these lines, it appeared to take after, depleting ill will or pushing out evil spirits or siphoning endlessly dark bile to bring the body once again into equalization must be great medication. Be it an expulsion or a purgative, the thought is the same: get the terrible stuff out and you'll come back to typical.

It's medication like, on the grounds that there are mind chemicals and other behavioral fortifications at work. On the off chance that you get usual to letting loose a little, you get to be subject to it.

Judgment skills says venting is an essential approach to simplicity pressure, yet sound judgment isn't right. Venting – purification – is emptying fuel into a flame.

While you absolutely would prefer not to disregard your issues, examines found that doing nothing was more powerful in enraging scatter than venting those disappointments. While it might feel great, venting just keeps the displeasure present.

Assess

In evaluating your issues, you have to discover somebody who will ensure you don't escape with horse crap. Aside from that individual, you additionally must be careful yourself and check what you're stating.

- When you feel activated, submit yourself to giving some time for the circumstance to prepare. At the end of the day, permit that prefrontal cortex to understand it all. Furious at a driver? You can pick not to follow up on your underlying response. Initial, a moment to simply inhale and let the minute pass.

- Don't form a hasty opinion. We are great at labeling circumstances and blaming others on a minute's notification. In any case, imagine a scenario where we just couldn't see the canine sitting in the street just before that auto that was taking so long to turn. Consider the possibility that their auto slowed down and they simply required a few moments to restart it. There are unlimited potential outcomes in the matter of "why" something simply happened and we might not have all the data we have to make an educated response. Work on staying at the time without marking and judging, i.e. care

- Whose business would it say it was in any case? On the off chance that somebody didn't accomplish something straightforwardly at you, is it truly your business to respond to it? Venture back and solicit yourself, "Is it appropriate to say that this is any from my business?" "Is there an answer for this issue and, assuming this is the case, who is capable?" Why do we invest so much energy getting our quills unsettled over things we see that don't include us?

- Attempt a contrasting option to venting boisterously. As opposed to hurrying off to an associate or yanking out that cell to prattle, snatch a pen and scribble down some notes or email yourself about what you're furious about. Scribbling down a few musings instead of gabbing every one of them over the workplace will connect with your body physically and rationally and permit your cerebrum to deplete to back off. Also, it makes for a friendlier office.

- In the event that you have to converse with somebody after you've attempted alternate thoughts, request that a trusted companion witness your venting and set breaking points.

Ask someone; "Could I converse with you for five minutes? What's more, I truly mean five!"

Next time you end up venting, pay consideration on how frequently you rehash the same data. Presumably a ton. When we're worked up we rehash ourselves for Emphasis. Setting points of confinement will drive us to keep it brief, sort out our considerations, and after that attention on to an answer.

Communicate and Empathize

These initial two stages are intended to clean up your brain since you need to go into the third one with clarity of thought. The third step is the point at which you converse with your supervisor. Work issues require correspondence with your chief, regardless of the possibility that that director is the issue.

The initial two stages guarantee you aren't a rambling clown when you request your manager's opportunity. When you begin talking, clarify your issues, propose arrangements, and see what they need to say. Be that as it may, above all, apologize. When you're demotivated, you are not doing your best work and your supervisor has likely seen, so apologize in the event that you believe it's essential.

It helps on the off chance that you know how to empathize you can be true about your statement of regret.

Why would it be advisable for you to unequivocally work to improve your capacity to relate to others? The following are some of the benefits of learning to empathize.

- You will probably treat the general population in a way that they would wish to be treated
- You will better comprehend the requirements of individuals around you.
- You will all the more plainly comprehend the recognition you make in others with your words and activities.
- You will comprehend the implicit parts of your correspondence with others.
- You will better comprehend the requirements of your clients at work.
- You will experience less difficulty managing interpersonal clash both at home and at work.
- You will also have the ability to, more precisely expect the activities and responses of individuals you cooperate with.
- You will figure out how to inspire the general population around you.
- You will all the more adequately persuade others regarding your perspective.
- You will encounter the world in higher determination as you see through your point of

view as well as the viewpoints of everyone around you.

- You will think that its less demanding to manage the antagonism of others in the event that you can better comprehend their inspirations and fears. Recently when I get myself expressly battling with somebody, I remind myself to identify I instantly quiet myself and acknowledge the circumstance for what it is.

When you learn to communicate your stress with empathy, it will make a world of a difference to you and also to the one you are talking to.

Chapter 4: The Infamous Rule of Three

This is a great way to motivate yourself if you dislike your job.

You can't snap your fingers and feel propelled once more. It requires investment to do the greater part of the above procedures. In the event that you don't have the privilege to enjoy a reprieve from work, utilize the rule of three.

Try not to mistake exercises for results. You're driving for three results (or results). This helps you ground your action against something significant for you. It likewise helps you concentrate on the end, not the methods. One of the most ideal approaches to get results is to stay adaptable in your methodology, while watching out for the prize.

The Rule of Three is an extremely straightforward approach to get results.

As opposed to get overpowered by your assignments, you pick Three things you need to accomplish. This places you in control. In the case of nothing else, it gives you an extremely straightforward edge for the day.

Three is Magic

Three is a fascinating number in children's stories. The military uses the standard of Three to educate survival:

- Three minutes away from air,
- Three days away from water,
- Three weeks away from food,
- Three months with no one to trust.

Three is the enchanted number.

Here is the way the Rule of Three applies to time:

- Three results for the day
- Three results for the week
- Three results for month
- Three results for the year

The results at every level backing each other and aide your outcomes.

Having Three results at every level (day, week, month, year) helps you see the timberland for the trees. To put it another way, your Three results for the year are greater than your Three results for the month, are greater than your Three results for the week, are greater than your Three results for the day.

Try not to mistake exercises for results. You're driving for Three results. This helps you ground your action against something significant for you. It likewise helps you concentrate on the end, not the methods. One of the most ideal approaches to get results is to stay adaptable in your methodology, while watching out for the prize.

In the event that you discover you become mixed up in your objectives or if your objectives are excessively mind boggling, attempt the tenet of Three. For instance;

- Get to battling weight
- Take an epic experience
- Ship a book

The results are straightforward dreams without bounds. You can encounter them and you can see them like a scene in a motion picture.

While these results are anything but difficult to say, there's a ton behind them.

For instance, getting to battling weight really incorporates things like having the capacity to do parts and hopping/turning kicks once more. In any case, "battling weight" is a basic analogy you can use to guide yourself consistently.

Basically, a result is the consequence of a cluster of exercises. So "have an incredible lunch with the group" is a result, yet for that, you have to perform a cluster of exercises like picking a spot and a period advantageous for everybody, ensuring it's a glad situation, and so forth.

Practicing It

- Begin your day with the standard of Three. When you wake up, list of Three things you want to achieve. Obviously, this may not be always possible but it will give you focus.

- Test yourself. What are the Three things you need to finish for the day? On the off chance that you need to find them, it's excessively muddled. In the event that your Three results are entangled, odds are they are truly exercises. Play around with how you say your Three results.

- Enhance your assessments. By paying consideration on your outcomes, you'll begin to make sense of to what extent things truly take you. You'll show signs of improvement at assessing both for the day and for the week. Recall that, you get the chance to hone every day, so you should simply focus and you'll move forward.

- When you end your day, take note of your Three achievements. It's a state of mind of appreciation that fabricates force. In the event that you didn't achieve the Three results you needed, then in any event you learned something. Either gnaw off littler lumps or attempt another methodology. Having Three achievements added to your repertoire is an even minded approach to like results.

Chapter 5: Take a Vacation Once in a While

Everybody longs for taking a vacation. Travel can get anybody energized when thinking about the sights you can see–the smells, the sustenance, the opportunity. Usually those longings break down into unfulfilled wishes turning into a far off dream you can't get a handle on. Numerous individuals do without vacations dreadfully long, regularly because of absence of time and cash.

A get-away doesn't should be expensive or long to have advantages. A moderate weekend show signs of improvement than none by any stretch of the imagination. The key is to completely unplug from work and the general unremarkable exercises of your life. This gives you a chance to energize your body and psyche which conveys exponential advantages, both short-and long haul.

Following as some advantages to taking a vacation.

Decompress – Discharge Stress and Stresses

We live in a world that is more quick paced and upsetting than any other time in recent memory. Work and home life requests, desires, and data over-burden keep on increasing.

Stress, is regularly the hidden guilty party behind generally sickness. We get so used to living at this upsetting pace we once in a while even acknowledge we're pushed or need a break.

Neglecting to recognize your body's requirement for a get-away can have tremendous expenses while leaving behind its numerous required advantages.

Energize Your Batteries

Restoration is above all else. Without it your wellbeing, work, and connections will pay the cost. Once more, albeit numerous individuals feel they don't have sufficient energy or cash to relax, in all actuality, they can't bear the cost of not to.

Taking a vacation is as essential as charging your wireless. Taking short breaks resemble charging your telephone for 5-10 minutes, it's useful yet not going to have much enduring impact. Relaxation and recreational time amid nights or weekends resemble charging your telephone for 20-Three0 minutes.

Enhance Relationships

Imparting time to family and companions without the diversions and day by day hassles of life makes delight and assembles affectionate recollections that bond. Individuals desire a feeling of having a place and get-away offers a connectedness not accomplished somewhere else.

A Vacation can likewise fortify relational unions, whether you go with your mate, or travel alone. Both choices are sound for relationships.

Improve Profitability

Numerous individuals report expanded efficiency, by and by and professionally, after a vacation. Edified laborers, including directors and supervisors, realize that the yield and main concern of an organization increment when representatives require some serious energy off. Expanded efficiency regularly compares into all the sparer time and more cash.

Build Clarity and Vision

Going on vacations regularly conveys clarity to critical thinking, imperative activities, or objectives. It likewise bolsters expanded vision. The negligible consequence of unwinding and restoration can suddenly convey a new view, replies, or significant bits of knowledge. This clarity may uncover itself amid or after your vacation.

Happiness

Research has indicated vacation to build serotonin (the glad hormone) and direct melatonin, circadian mood, and rest cycles. It besides can diminish cortisol generation, decreasing anxiety, which likewise makes a more satisfied individual.

Arranging an excursion and anticipating it is said to expand energy and joy for a considerable length of time to weeks paving the way to the get-away. In this way it is sharp to begin arranging another excursion soon after you return. Along these lines you can persistently surf the highs of the suspicion of your next excursion!

Secondary Advantages: Leading by an Example

In case you're a guardian, instructor, administrator, or supervisor you won't just benefit yourself by vacationing (regardless of how bustling you will be)— you will likewise help other people figure out how to do it. Numerous individuals demonstrate the previously stated parts, whether coincidentally or deliberately, and it is accordingly vital to show others how it's done.

It's essential to note that the advantages to your family, collaborators, or associates will much of the time stream over to you. At the point when individuals deal with themselves, they are more satisfied. More satisfied individuals are less demanding to identify with—period.

Being an upbeat revived individual has numerous advantages, seen and concealed, to your own and expert life. Moreover, expanded efficiency combined with recently discovered clarity and vision can prompt a salary increase, additional time off, "work from home" open doors, and a great deal more.

It's about being more viable, upbeat, and healthy—all a result of traveling.

Conclusion

Thank you again for purchasing this book!

It's difficult to continue going when you're feeling demotivated, however ideally, these tips ought to help you push on. Try not to confound an absence of inspiration with burnout, which is a genuine issue.

I trust this book could help you guzzle the right outlook expected to help you in overcoming demotivation at work and at last make you more productive. The following stride is to manage the positive changes you have set aside a few minutes and keep donning a proactive mentality in underscoring the fundamental part you play at the work environment.

Try not to think little of the significance of dealing with yourself. It's anything but difficult to feel like each employment sucks if the issue is really with you. For instance, in case you're clinically discouraged and even the things that typically bring you satisfaction fall down.

In case you're not getting enough rest, or your eating regimen needs some help, your mentality and way to deal with your whole day, at work or at home, will be affected. Exercise, rest, time with loved ones, and looking after your mental and physical prosperity as a rule all come way towards making any employment more endurable.

Finally, if you enjoyed this book, please take the time to share your thoughts and post a review on Amazon. It'd be greatly appreciated!

Thank you and good luck!

54443822R00027

Made in the USA
Middletown, DE
03 December 2017